Career Discovery

Careers If You Like Sports

Stuart A. Kallen

ReferencePoint Press®

San Diego, CA

About the Author
Stuart A. Kallen is the author of more than 350 nonfiction books for children and young adults. He has written on topics ranging from the theory of relativity to the art of electronic dance music. In addition, Kallen has written award-winning children's videos and television scripts. In his spare time he is a singer, songwriter, and guitarist in San Diego.

For more information, contact:
ReferencePoint Press, Inc.
PO Box 27779
San Diego, CA 92198
www.ReferencePointPress.com

Photo credits:
Cover: iStockphoto/ranplett
10: iStockphoto/Steve Cole Images
16: iStockphoto.com/Steve Debenport
27: iStockphoto/CasarsaGuru
57: iStockphoto.com/Steve Cole Images

LIBRARY OF CONGRESS CATALOGING-IN-PUBLICATION DATA

Names: Kallen, Stuart A., 1955– author.
Title: Careers If You Like Sports/by Stuart A. Kallen.
Description: San Diego, CA: ReferencePoint Press, Inc., 2018. | Series: Career Discovery | Includes bibliographical references and index.
Identifiers: LCCN 2017023856 (print) | LCCN 2017026079 (ebook) | ISBN 9781682821435 (eBook) | ISBN 9781682821428 (hardback)
Subjects: LCSH: Sports—Vocational guidance—Juvenile literature.
Classification: LCC GV734 (ebook) | LCC GV734 .K35 2018 (print) | DDC 796.023—dc23
LC record available at https://lccn.loc.gov/2017023856

CONTENTS

Introduction: An Industry-Wide Hiring Binge

In 2017 there were about eighteen thousand professional baseball, basketball, football, ice hockey, tennis, soccer, and other players and athletes in the United States. According to the National Collegiate Athletic Association (NCAA) more than 480,000 college athletes compete to join the professional ranks every year. Who can blame them? Many professional athletes are rich and famous, and millions of people regard them as heroes. But even for the athletically inclined, the odds of becoming a professional athlete are slim. According to the NCAA, only one out of every 2,451 high school basketball players will ever play on a National Basketball Association (NBA) team. In all sports but baseball, the chances of going from college to a professional team are less than 2 percent; about 11 percent of college baseball players make it into the major leagues.

Maybe the idea of breaking down those numbers and compiling mathematical data about sports, athletes, and teams inspires you more than throwing a basketball or baseball does. If you love the game but tend to be more agile with a calculator, you might be interested in becoming a sports statistician. People who work in this field use their math and computer skills to analyze sports statistics to provide insight into athletic performances.

The job of statistician is one of many nonathletic professions that involve the sports industry. Some who pursue careers in the sports industry have medical backgrounds and work as doctors, trainers, nutritionists, or therapists. Those who want to spend their time on the playing field work as coaches, referees, fitness directors, trainers, facility managers, or general managers. The fastest-growing sectors of the industry—media and marketing—employ thousands of journalists, broadcasters, producers, website administrators, and sales and public relations representatives.

The sports industry is flourishing—this economic sector was projected to generate $68 billion in revenue in 2017. Indeed, the industry is on what can only be described as a hiring binge, even as the number of teams has remained constant. "The addition of jobs created by the growth of technology—from system engineering, to analytics and social media—has opened up thousands of additional positions that did not exist a decade ago," explains sportswriter Jason Belzer. "Moreover, the influx of billions in television and sponsorship dollars . . . has allowed for the proliferation of sports marketing, management and consulting agencies . . . [searching for] top talent."[1]

Sports Education Programs

These days, most desirable job candidates need a college degree in sports medicine, statistics, programming, management, or marketing. As a result, the number of colleges that offer undergraduate and master's courses in sports-related subjects has exploded in recent decades. Consider that in 1985 there were just three colleges with sports education programs; by 2017, there were more than three hundred.

Some of the most prestigious sports-related graduate programs include the DeVos Sport Business Management Program at the University of Central Florida, the Mark H. McCormack Department of Sport Management at UMass Amherst, and Rutgers University global sports business program. According to the SportBusiness International postgraduate sports course rankings, Ohio University's Center for Sports Administration earned the title of #1 Overall Postgraduate Sports Course. More than 85 percent of the university's fourteen hundred graduates work in key positions in intercollegiate athletics, professional sports, sports tours, corporate sports organizations, and the sports media industry.

Internships and Conferences

Students can improve their chances of entering a top-rated sports education program by doing an internship. There are numerous agencies, organizations, and institutions in the sports industry that hire interns every semester. The competition for these internships can be almost as tough as competing for a spot on a professional team. However, obtaining an internship is important for anyone wishing to work in the industry. According to Carolyne Savini, vice president of recruiting at Turnkey Sports & Entertainment: "For anyone trying to break into the sports industry at the entry level, internship experience is critical. Short of an inside connection, I rarely, if ever, see someone get hired into a job without previous internship experience."[2]

Some find internships through online listings. But there are numerous sports-related conferences and job fairs where students can network, learn about the industry, and make connections to obtain internship positions. The National Sports Forum is the nation's largest gathering of top executives in sports sales, promotions, marketing, and entertainment. The University of Michigan Sports Business Conference is a student-run gathering that features more than twenty-five leading sports industry guest speakers. The Ivy Sports Symposium rotates among Ivy League schools. This large conference has more than one hundred guest speakers along with breakout sessions and panel discussions geared toward students seeking careers in the industry.

Professional athletes must have a single-minded focus on their sport. They must be willing to sacrifice many of life's comforts to thrive. While job seekers in the sports industry do not have to work quite that hard, it takes grit and determination to go the distance in an industry that attracts countless contenders.

Athletic Trainer

A Few Facts

Median Salary

$45,630 per year in 2016

Minimum Educational Requirements

Bachelor's degree in athletic training

Personal Qualities

Compassionate, studious, detail oriented, sports lover, good decision-making and communication skills, physically fit

Working Conditions

Indoors in gyms and outdoors on playing fields

Number of Jobs

24,500 in 2016

Job Outlook

Expected to grow 21 percent through 2024

What Does an Athletic Trainer Do?

Casey Riley is an athletic trainer (AT) at the high school level who works with a girls' basketball team in Danville, Kentucky. Most people think she makes her living taping sprained ankles—and athletic trainers sometimes do bandage the ankles of injured players. But Riley says that wrapping ankles is just one small part of an athletic trainer's job: "I take care of athletes from beginning to end. From making sure . . . the practice area they are on is safe, and even if the environment is suitable for practice and games. On top of that, I also deal with injuries from when they happen, through some rehab depending on the injury, to return to play (which can include taping depending on the injury)."[3]

Athletic training is recognized by the American Medical Association (AMA) as a health care profession. The job should not be confused with fitness trainer or personal trainer; those people train others to become physically fit but are not health care workers.

Athletic trainers use their knowledge of nutrition, hygiene, conditioning, sports psychology, and protective equipment to keep athletes safe and ensure they are performing to the best of their ability. The overriding goal of an athletic trainer is to prevent injuries by implementing training regimens that are steeped in education and prevention. When injuries occur during a game, athletic trainers are usually the first medical personnel on the scene. They provide first aid and emergency care on the playing field and consult with the team physician to diagnose and treat a player's injuries. Athletic trainers also design rehabilitation programs and work one-on-one with athletes to help them get back in the game.

Athletic trainers who are not employed by professional sports teams must be skilled at working with people of all abilities and ages. They need to have a solid understanding of pain tolerance and recognize appropriate treatment options for clients based on their age.

A Typical Day on the Job

Athletic trainers work forty to fifty hours a week during the off-season and up to seventy hours a week when a team's sport is in season. They might split their time between clinics, patient services, and the various teams for which they work. Athletic trainers who work with high school teams regularly work after school hours from around 2 to 6 p.m.

In the morning, an athletic trainer might work with a physician in a sports medicine clinic prepping and suturing wounds, removing stitches, and setting casts, braces, and splints. During the midafternoon, he or she might be scheduling tests and exercise programs for patients while answering questions and offering counseling. Depending on the situation, athletic trainers meet with the team physician several times a week or every day. They likely discuss specific injuries and treatment options and perform evaluations.

In season, hours vary depending on the number of practices and games scheduled. Riley claims she is never off the clock during basketball season. She might start work with her players at 9:30 a.m. and still be up at 1 a.m. answering texts and phone messages from athletes who are just getting back from away games. Riley describes a weekend in March 2017 when her basketball team participated in the Kentucky state championship: "Just Saturday and Sunday alone, my schedule included a shoot-around practice, pregame taping, 6:30 p.m. game, post-game treatment (ice baths), handing out ice bags at 10 p.m. at the hotel, injury treatment at 9:30 a.m. then a game and it all starts again at 2 p.m."[4]

While athletic trainers are most often associated with team sports, they also work with dancers and musicians who have physically demanding jobs. Katie Lemmon works as an athletic trainer with respected dance companies like the Joffrey Ballet and DanceWorks Chicago. She also works for the Chicago Bulls cheerleading squad and the team's Luvabulls dance company. In addition, Lemmon gives lectures on injury prevention. Key to her job is becoming intimately familiar with each athlete's individual injuries and physical tendencies. As she says of her duties with the Joffrey Ballet:

I get to know the dancers very well and . . . often assess their dance technique to get to the bottom of what may be causing their injury rather than just "putting a Band-Aid" on

9

An athletic trainer assists an injured football player. Athletic trainers are first responders when injuries occur on the playing field. They also design rehabilitation programs and work with athletes to help them get back in the game.

the injury or treating the symptoms. If a dancer is injured during a performance, I get called backstage. I assess the injury in the "wings" and make a quick decision, hopefully helping them return to the stage.[5]

How Do You Become an Athletic Trainer?

Athletic trainers are highly qualified medical professionals. Students interested in this career should focus on math, biology, chemistry, physics, first aid, nutrition, and other health- and medical-related subjects. They will also need to get a bachelor's degree in athletic training from an accredited institution. Programs to focus on include therapeutic procedures, injury and illness prevention, and first aid and emergency care. Instruction in human anatomy and physiology helps students learn about the human body and its muscular, circulatory, and skeletal systems. Classroom studies are supplemented with hands-on clinical experience, which might include dissecting human cadavers.

Some athletic trainers study kinesiology, the science of human movement. Kinesiology students learn how various exercise programs affect the body, especially the muscles and skeletal system. Kinesiology also looks at the way injuries can be caused by actions made during different types of sports. Some students also take courses in sports psychology, which help students learn motivational techniques and ways to psychologically support injured and recuperating athletes. The psychology of sports also focuses on how exercise and training practices can affect a player's emotional health and well-being. Finally, athletic trainers are required to understand sports nutrition and ways different types of food, vitamins, and supplements enhance athletic performance and influence overall health.

A bachelor's degree is a minimum requirement to work as an athletic professional; more than 75 percent of those working in the field have a master's degree or higher. A master's degree opens up career opportunities and opportunities to advance, especially at colleges and universities. According to a 2017 statement by the Commission on Accreditation of Athletic Training Education, professional athletic training programs will soon offer only master's programs.

Before they can practice in the field, those who have degrees in athletic training are required to pass the Board of Certification for the athletic trainer exam. Athletic trainers must also be credentialed in the state in which they practice. In addition, because most positions in high schools involve teaching, a teaching certificate or license could be required.

Personality and Skills

Most athletic trainers are sports lovers who are competitive by nature. They share the athlete's love of the game and understand their desire to recover as quickly as possible. Teamwork is a requirement for anyone who works in sports, and athletic trainers must be skilled team players. Athletic trainers often serve as role models for athletes and need to maintain a positive attitude and keep morale high. They should be willing to form close personal relationships with coaches, players, administrators, physicians, and other health care professionals. On many occasions, athletic trainers also consult with parents and relatives of players. Finally, the job is physically demanding so athletic trainers need to be in good shape.

Good communication skills are a must for athletic trainers. They need to speak clearly to players, be able to assess their performance and injuries, and communicate detailed information about training programs. Playing a sport can be stressful, especially when injuries occur. Therefore, athletic trainers need to remain levelheaded and speak in calm, measured tones to athletes, especially those who are experiencing pain and frustration. Athletic trainers should also be prepared to experience personal stress; they are often called on to make quick decisions that could affect the long-term health or career of their clients.

Working Conditions

Depending on what they specialize in, athletic trainers work either indoors or outdoors. They typically work with medical equipment and machinery and are often required to stand for long periods of time. Athletic trainers walk and run around playing fields and kneel, crouch, stoop, and even crawl while treating injured players.

In National Collegiate Athletic Association Division I colleges and universities, athletic trainers generally work at least fifty to sixty hours a week with one team. Travel is often required. Those who work at smaller colleges and universities often teach and work with several teams. Athletic trainers with professional sports teams work the longest hours, spending up to twelve hours a day at training camps, practices, and games.

Who's Hiring?

Athletic trainers work in clinical, athletic, and educational settings. They are seen in gyms and on playing fields at community centers, high schools, colleges, and universities. Athletic trainers are also employed by professional sports teams, sports medicine clinics, health clubs, and hospitals. Some work with dance companies, while others are hired by individuals to run personalized training programs. Many athletic trainers also give speeches at educational institutions.

Career Advancement

There are several ways athletic trainers can move their career forward. An assistant athletic trainer can advance to become a head athletic trainer, and eventually athletic director. Athletic trainers can also become part of a physician group practice, where they might manage other trainers. Some use their background in athletic training to go on to sell medical or athletic equipment or move into marketing positions.

What Is the Future Outlook for Athletic Trainers?

According to figures compiled by the Bureau of Labor Statistics (BLS), around 25,400 people worked as athletic trainers in 2016 for an average pay of $45,630 a year. The job outlook is good; people are becoming more aware of the harm caused by sports-related injuries and ways to prevent them. This will lead to an increased demand for athletic trainers. The BLS says employment of athletic trainers is expected to grow 21 percent by 2024.

Find Out More

Board of Certification (BOC) for the Athletic Trainer
1415 Harney St., Suite 200
Omaha, NE 68102
http://bocatc.org

This organization was established in 1989 to provide credentialed certification to entry-level athletic training professionals. The BOC website contains a wealth of information for prospective athletic trainers, including education and job placement resources and certification requirements in all fifty states.

Commission on Accreditation of Athletic Training Education
6850 Austin Center Blvd., Suite 100
Austin, TX 78731
http://caate.net

This organization is in charge of accrediting athletic training programs in the United States. The commission's website contains information students can use to learn about becoming an athletic trainer, accreditation instructions, and professional and residency programs.

National Athletic Trainers' Association
1620 Valwood Pkwy., Suite 115
Carrollton, TX 75006
www.nata.org

This professional membership association is for certified athletic trainers. The organization's website features a careers and education section that has a variety of resources pertaining to training, job placement, practice and patient care, and professional development.

Professional Football Athletic Trainers Society (PFATS)
www.pfats.com

The PFATS represents athletic trainers in the National Football League (NFL). The website contains information about the work performed by professional football athletic trainers, while the Career Zone section provides educational information about degree and certification programs, NFL internships, and paths to become a credentialed NFL athletic trainer.

Coach

What Does a Coach Do?

Some coaches reach the same status as celebrities and rock stars. Professional football head coaches like Pete Carroll of the Seattle Seahawks and Sean Payton of the New Orleans Saints each earned around $8 million in 2017. Their faces are familiar to millions of fans, as are the details of their careers. While coaches in professional basketball, baseball, and soccer do not earn as much, the job can be financially rewarding. Of course, most coaches are not rich and famous. Thousands of men and women who coach sports teams are not motivated by money, but by a love of what they do. They earn a modest salary coaching at middle schools, high schools, and colleges.

Most coaches view themselves first and foremost as educators. They direct, instruct, and train individual athletes and teams. Coaches teach sportsmanship, game strategies, and playing techniques. They plan and supervise practice sessions and oversee physical conditioning programs that help athletes perform to the best of their abilities. Coaches analyze their players' and teams' strengths and weaknesses and do the same with opponents.

15

A soccer coach gives players a pep talk before a game. The job of a coach is to direct, instruct, and train athletes. Coaches also teach sportsmanship, game strategies, and playing techniques in addition to developing winning game plans.

Coaches must develop game plans that feature winning strategies. Game plans outline what positions athletes will play and provide instructions for them to follow. During games coaches call specific plays meant to surprise or overwhelm their opponents. They also decide when to send in substitute players who might have a better chance of achieving success. Coaches are also in charge of keeping their players safe. They establish safety procedures and do their best to ensure that players do not sustain concussions and other injuries, or suffer from heat stroke or dehydration.

Coaches also act as mentors. They inspire their players to work hard, set goals, develop skills, and swing for the stars. High school football coach Ted Kimmey, who works in Satellite Beach, Florida, takes pride in helping his athletes win games while developing their character. "Leadership can be developed in every single person, and I'm fascinated by the whole leadership process. I think a lot of coaches say they want to develop men or adults. We've kind of changed that here," says Kimmey. "One of my main missions is that we want to develop leaders, people who go on and change the world."[6]

Some coaches also work as scouts. They look for new players, evaluate their skills, and assess their ability to compete at the amateur, college, or professional level. Scouts recruit new players and offer incentives to join their team. This part of the job involves reading about promising athletes in the news, attending games, studying a player's statistics, and watching videos of their performances.

Most coaches are not in the business of recruiting the best athletes. Rather, their job is to develop the athletic potential of students who happen to attend the school where they work. While training student athletes to compete can be rewarding, coaches must be prepared to deal with losses, too. Defeat causes stress, frustration, and anger not only in athletes, but among parents and fans. Sometimes, this anger is directed at the coach. As such, coaches are often publicly criticized, which can be difficult. "Coaching is . . . an occupation that is most often done in a public fishbowl," says sports consultant Alan Goldberg. "You are in a highly visible position that continually exposes you to the public's scrutiny and evaluation. It's one of those professions where the general public regularly weighs in on what kind of a job they think you're doing whether you want their evaluation or not."[7]

How Do You Become a Coach?

Most coaches are driven by their love of sports. Many began their careers coaching a children's sports league. At this level, candidates are hired based on their basic knowledge of the sport and its rules. Coaches in youth sports are often required to pass background checks to ensure the safety of the children they are supervising. While an applicant's traffic tickets might be overlooked, those with DWIs, serious misdemeanors, or long rap sheets can forget their dreams of becoming a children's coach.

Those who wish to coach in secondary and postsecondary institutions need to get a bachelor's degree. Coaches typically hold degrees in sports leadership or sports science. Others major

Teacher, Role Model, and Communicator

"As football coaches, we're so good at talking Xs and Os, but . . . I've really tried to focus hard, in this program, on understanding who we are, what are we trying to achieve and then apply it. We've kind of put an emphasis on being a teacher, a role model, communicator, a person who develops kids and then the football stuff later. You can learn (football), but the other stuff is hard."

—Ted Kimmey, head football coach, Satellite High, Satellite Beach, Florida

Quoted in Brian McCallum, "Q&A: New Satellite High Football Coach Ted Kimmey," *Florida Today*, April 17, 2017. www.floridatoday.com.

in physical education or leisure studies. These programs focus on sports psychology, conditioning and fitness training, coaching technology, coaching theory and methods, and officiating sports.

Those interested in a career as a coach can go on to earn a master's degree in sports coaching. Master's courses focus on coaching research methods, leadership principles, sports administration, sports medicine and injury prevention, and sports law. College coaches often also teach in a classroom, which requires them to hold a master's degree or higher in whatever courses they teach.

Most states require coaches to be certified, which means they must be trained in cardiopulmonary resuscitation and first aid. Coaches might also be required to take sports safety and coaching fundamentals classes. The United States Sports Academy offers a National Coaching Certification Program that features classroom training in coaching techniques, ethics, sports administration, coaching methodology, nutrition, injury prevention, and sports psychology. Individual courses focus on coaching track and field, cross-country, volleyball, tennis, softball, basketball, baseball, football, and soccer. Students can pursue four levels of coaching certification. Additional certification may be required in some states to become an instructor in scuba diving, tennis, golf, karate, or other individual sports.

Personality and Skills

Coaches need leadership skills to motivate, develop, and direct young athletes. Being an effective leader requires one to have good communication skills. Coaches use these skills when they instruct, organize, and motivate athletes, and when they call out concise strategies, game plans, and plays over the roar of the crowd. Part of being a good communicator involves listening. Coaches who listen to their athletes often use suggestions from players to improve playing strategies and team performance. Secondary school coaches also need to take time to connect with athletes' families. "Make it a regular practice to communicate with the parents and educate them about the sport and the role that they need to play on the team," recommends Goldberg. "Teach [parents] what are appropriate and inappropriate behaviors at games and on the sidelines. . . . Explain your philosophy about competition and playing time."[8]

Coaches also need to provide assurance, encouragement, and positive feedback to both athletes and parents. Patience is an important quality when dealing with frustrated athletes and angry fans. It helps to have a sense of humor, especially when things get stressful or tense—as coaches always say, "it's only a game." That said, the importance placed on winning can raise issues that coaches need to be prepared to handle. A good coach never embarrasses or humiliates players for their mistakes or failures. Additionally, coaches need to keep their egos in check; the game is not about them. Whatever its outcome, the overriding goal is to teach athletes positive life lessons.

Working Conditions

Coaches work on playing fields, in gyms, and at pools. They may work indoors and outdoors depending on the sport. Those who coach sports that are held outdoors may be exposed to all sorts of weather conditions, including extreme heat, cold, rain, and snow. They are often required to travel to sporting events in buses or airplanes. Many middle and high school coaches are also teachers or administrators who coach more than one sport. Full-time coaches usually work for more than forty hours a week for several months during the sport's season, and the job includes irregular hours including evenings, weekends, and holidays. Shawn Windle, a training coach for the Indiana Pacers, describes the effect his job has on his family: "With all the travel and home games included I missed 110 dinners and bedtimes at home, causing my wife to function as a single parent from October until April."[9]

Who's Hiring?

Elementary and secondary schools hire the largest number of sports coaches. According to the Bureau of Labor Statistics (BLS) the average salary for those positions was $31,000 annually in 2015. Most coaching jobs are in football, baseball, basketball, soccer, lacrosse, wrestling, and track and field. Positions include high school head coach, college head coach, and assistant coach. Those who work as personal sports instructors with individual athletes can earn up to $70,050 annually.

Career Advancement

Most college coaches begin their careers as assistant coaches, and gain a lot of knowledge and experience in these positions. High school coaches can sometimes advance to the college level, and from there rise up to the professional ranks if they have a lot of experience and a winning record. Jill Ellis, head coach of the US women's national soccer team, offers the following advice to those looking to make a career in coaching: "Don't be in a rush, make sure you're prepared, and surround yourself with people that you can learn and grow from," she says. "Even as a college coach, I would watch what other people did. It made me think of something new or look at something with a different perspective."[10]

Some who are trained in the fundamentals of coaching and

team sports become freelance sports instructors. This work is similar to coaching, but involves more one-on-one work with athletes or individuals who simply want to improve their skills. Sports instructors teach skills that are specific to individual sports, and might coach baseball players in pitching or teach tennis, golf, skiing, or karate.

What Is the Future Outlook for Coaches?

According to a *U.S. News & World Report* survey, sports coaching ranks sixth on a 2017 list of best education jobs. The BLS projects a 6 percent growth for sports coaches through 2024. This means about 14,800 new positions for sports coaches will be added to the 250,600 professionals already working in the field. Much of the growth will occur in high school sports, as student enrollment is expected to increase over the next decade. As more students fill classrooms, a greater number of student athletes will work with coaches as they participate in football, volleyball, basketball, and other sports.

There will be a similar uptick in college sports. The BLS predicts this will be especially true at smaller Division III colleges, which are expected to add new teams and expand their sports programs to attract more students. Women's sports will have the most opportunities for coaches; according to government figures, female participation in high school and college sports has exploded, growing 50 percent a year.

Find Out More

National Alliance for Youth Sports
2050 Vista Pkwy.
West Palm Beach, FL 33411
www.nays.org

This organization focuses on education and training youth sports coaches, many of whom are volunteers. The website focuses on topics that coaches of all sports need to know, such as working with parents, motivating kids, building confidence, safety, and nutrition.

National High School Coaches Association
1 S. Third St., Suite 812
Easton, PA 18042
www.nhsca.com

This organization caters to the professional needs of high school coaches. The website offers membership to non-coaches and features numerous links to educational programs and information of interest to prospective coaches.

National Soccer Coaches Association of America (NSCAA)
30 W. Pershing Rd., Suite 350
Kansas City, MO 64108
www.nscaa.com

The NSCAA is the world's largest soccer coaches' organization. The website features details about soccer coaching education, a coaching career guide, internship programs, and job listings.

Positive Coaching Alliance
1001 N. Rengstorff Ave., Suite 100
Mountain View, CA 94043
www.positivecoach.org

This organization focuses on providing positive sports experiences for youth and high school coaches, parents, and athletes. The website features numerous free educational multimedia resources containing tips and tools related to positive coaching.

Sports Physical Therapist

A Few Facts

Median Salary
$85,400 a year in 2016 for all physical therapists

Minimum Educational Requirements
A postgraduate doctor of physical therapy degree

Personal Qualities
Compassion, passion for sports, dexterity, physical strength, attention to detail, patience, communication skills

Working Conditions
Indoors at medical facilities, athletic clinics, and schools; outdoors in sports venues; irregular hours including evenings, weekends, and holidays; travel sometimes required

Number of Jobs
210,900 people worked in physical therapy in 2014

Job Outlook
Expected to grow 34 percent through 2024

What Does a Sports Physical Therapist Do?

Physical therapists work with people who suffer from severe injuries. These medical professionals, often referred to as PTs, work in hospitals, clinics, nursing homes, and private homes to help patients regain physical movement and manage pain. Like many health care professions, the field of physical therapy can be broken down into various niches, or specialties. One specialty is sports physical therapy, in which practitioners work with athletes who have been injured during games, practice, or training. The objective of a sports physical therapist is to help athletes recuperate as quickly as possible while ensuring that their recovery regimen does not cause further problems. Sports physical therapists also implement safe playing practices that help athletes avoid injuries before they occur.

Sports physical therapists help athletes with sprains, muscle strains (pulled muscles), fractures, torn ligaments, tendinitis, concussions, and other conditions caused by training and competing. They commonly attend to injuries of the back, neck, shoulders, knees, ankles, wrists, and elbows. During the course of their work, sports physical therapists work as part of a health care team, overseeing the work of PT assistants and aides and regularly consulting with physicians and surgeons.

Healing Patients

Doctors typically prescribe physical therapy to injured patients. When a patient is referred, a sports physical therapist will meet with the athlete and evaluate what treatments are necessary. The athlete typically describes the injury, explains how it occurred, what physical problems it causes, and what medications are being used to treat it. The sports PT will also ask about the athlete's current psychological state and past medical history.

The second phase of treatment involves making a diagnosis using two common physical therapy tools. One is an instrument called a goniometer, which has been in use for decades. It measures the range of motion in the knee, elbow, and other joints. In recent years the goniometer has been replaced by smartphone apps like Goniometer Pro, which have been shown to be just as accurate when calculating the angle of movement within a joint. Sports physical therapists can also use something as simple as a tape measure to determine how much swelling or muscle loss has occurred due to an injury.

Then, the sports physical therapist diagnoses the injury and analyzes issues concerning strength, balance, and health of the neuromuscular (nerve and muscle) systems. He or she uses this information to create a list of short- and long-term recovery goals. The recovery program can last from a few days for minor sprains to a few months for major injuries. It is designed to rehabilitate, or heal, the athlete. There is also a focus on "prehab," or what steps can be taken to prevent further injuries.

During treatment, a sports physical therapist has four main goals. The first is to decrease pain through manual techniques like massage or by applying hot or cold compresses. The second involves increasing the range of motion in an injured limb or joint. This is accomplished by prescribing an exercise program. Sports physical therapists might also employ therapeutic ultrasound, which features ultra-high-frequency sound waves to stimulate the tissue beneath the skin. Range-of-motion issues can also be treated using hydrotherapy, which involves soaking the injury in hot or cold water to stimulate the muscles.

As pain subsides and range of motion returns, a sports physical therapist will work to build an athlete's strength using free weights, weight resistance machines, and other weight training methods. During the final phase of treatment the sports physical therapist employs various techniques to improve an athlete's agility, reaction time, speed, and coordination in preparation for return to competition.

When they are not working with patients, sports physical therapists spend time reading, researching, and otherwise updating their knowledge. The field is constantly evolving as therapists and doctors discover new ways to prevent injuries and get athletes back in the game.

How Do You Become a Sports Physical Therapist?

High school students who set their sights on becoming sports physical therapists should focus on biology, chemistry, physics, and psychology. Undergraduate college students planning to apply to physical therapy school should major in sports medicine, which could include bachelor of science degrees in exercise and sport science, kinesiology, and athletic training. These majors give students an excellent scientific background in exercise and rehabilitation. Internship programs also play an important role according to doctor Jon Herting. "While in undergrad you should also seek out internships in strength and conditioning and sports performance settings in order to further your knowledge in the field," he says. "This [will] help you to excel in PT school and provide good connections and mentors that will serve you further down the road."[11]

Some schools offer undergraduate degrees known as 3+3 programs. In these, students are admitted to a graduate program in physical therapy when they begin college as an undergraduate. If students maintain a certain grade average for the first three years of their undergraduate education, they can begin their three-year graduate PT program during their senior undergrad year, saving a year of schooling (and the expenses that go along with it).

All states require physical therapists to be licensed. Requirements vary from state to state, but all physical therapists must pass the National Physical Therapy Examination administered by the Federation of State Boards of Physical Therapy. Many states require practitioners to undergo a criminal background check. Continuing education is also required for physical therapists to keep their license. Professional teams require physical therapists to become athletic trainer certified. The American Board of Physical Therapy Specialties provides sports certification for physical therapists.

Personality and Skills

Like most medical providers, sports physical therapists need to be compassionate. They spend their days helping people who are in pain, and thus must have patience and sympathy. The physical part of the job requires strength and endurance; sports physical therapists spend much of their day on their feet and need to be strong enough to lift patients, move their limbs, and assist in weight training. The job also requires manual dexterity to massage patients and help them exercise.

The job also requires a fair degree of creativity and attention to detail. Practitioners need to closely observe and analyze injuries, evaluate treatment regimens, and keep meticulous notes on a patient's progress. Sports physical therapists use this information to design customized treatment programs, which require that a practitioner be resourceful and flexible. Communication skills are important for clearly explaining treatment programs, motivating patients, and listening to their concerns. The job also requires dedication and commitment—not only to helping athletes at all levels, but for continually reading and learning about new treatments and therapies.

An injured athlete undergoes physical therapy. The sports physical therapist's goal is to help the athlete recuperate quickly and completely and provide techniques for avoiding future injury.

Working Conditions

Sports physical therapists work indoors in medical facilities, athletic clinics, and schools, and outdoors in sports venues. While most practitioners keep forty-hour work weeks, those who have positions on professional teams may work more demanding or irregular schedules that require them to travel and work on weekends and holidays. This requires the practitioner to have a great degree of passion about the sport. As sports physical therapist with the Boston Red Sox, Mike Reinold explains, "Many people don't realize how challenging sports medicine is as a profession. You need to be energetic, compassionate, patient, and love to interact with people. People also don't often realize what a normal work day is like. I work 12-hour days, 7-days a week, for 9 straight months. I am not kidding or exaggerating, check out a baseball schedule, there are no days off. Even on our off-days we have treatments and have to prepare for upcoming games."[12]

They Are Going to Test You

"I think you first have to identify what sport you are passionate about. I loved baseball ever since I was a kid. So in terms of a physical therapist's point of view . . . you want to be able to understand the physical demands of the sport and what the common type of injuries are associated with that sport. Obviously in baseball, elbows and shoulders get injured a lot of time. So you want to be able to have a firm understanding of that, because . . . in a job interview . . . they are going to test you and they are going to find out what your knowledge is."

—Jeff Cavaliere, sports physical therapist with the New York Mets

Quoted in Nitin Chhoda, "Physical Therapy Interview—Star Physical Therapist Jeff Cavaliere," Nitin360, June 23, 2009. https://nitin360.com.

Who's Hiring?

Sports physical therapists work for doctors, sports clinics, and minor and major league sports teams. Some are freelancers who take on individual clients. Reinold advanced his career by seeking out the best doctors in baseball. He went to work as a research assistant with one respected baseball physician, and within five years progressed to Director of Rehabilitation at the doctor's clinic. This made Reinold desirable to baseball teams.

Networking is also important when seeking employment. "The more you can network and join associations or attend conferences with people that are in a position that you want to be in one day, the better," says Reinold. "Look for mentors, look for friends, and look for opportunities. . . . Seek out the professional sports medicine association of the sport you are interested in. . . . Nothing beats experience, so the more specific your experience can be the better."[13]

Career Advancement

Some sports physical therapists begin their careers by volunteering for high school or minor league teams. This experience can lead to landing a job with a major league team. However, competition is tough in the big leagues; there are only several hundred major league teams and each team might hire only one or two full-time physical therapists.

Mark Kaufman, founder of Athletico Physical Therapy, found another way to advance his career. In college at the University of Iowa, Kaufman quickly discovered he wasn't good enough to play baseball. But he loved the game and understood athletes' needs, and so he became an athletic trainer who went on to pursue a career as a sports athletic therapist. He opened his first clinic in Chicago in 1991. The clinic was a success and Kaufman continued to open new clinics in other cities. In 2017 he owned 350 Athletico Physical Therapy facilities in nine states. Entrepreneurs like Kaufman might craft their own career path by opening their own practice like he did.

Salary and Future Outlook for Sports Physical Therapists?

About 210,900 people worked as physical therapists in 2014; the Bureau of Labor Statistics does not keep track of how many specialize in sports. The BLS says the average annual pay for all physical therapists was $85,400 in 2016. In addition, the field for all physical therapists is growing very quickly; 34 percent through 2024. Growth is fueled by a government rule implemented in 2015 called Direct Access. This allows patients in all fifty states and the District of Columbia to seek treatment from a licensed physical therapist without first obtaining a prescription or referral from a doctor. Direct Access saves patients time and money and is expected to increase the number of people who obtain physical therapy rather than physician care.

Find Out More

American Board of Physical Therapy Specialties
1111 N. Fairfax St.
Alexandria, VA 22314
www.abpts.org

This organization provides certification for PT specialists. The site's Sports Certification section contains applications, instructional videos, and eligibility guidelines.

American Orthopaedic Society for Sports Medicine
9400 W. Higgins Rd., Suite 300
Rosemont, IL 60018
www.sportsmed.org

This organization is dedicated to sports medicine education, research, and communication and works closely with athletic trainers, physical therapists, and others to identify, prevent, and treat sports injuries. The website offers online education, fellowships, and other resources of interest to those interested in sports physical therapy.

American Physical Therapy Association
1111 N. Fairfax St.
Alexandria, VA 22314
www.apta.org

The association represents physical therapists, physical therapist assistants, and students of physical therapy. The Practice & Patient Care section of the website covers many aspects of the physical therapy business, while the Careers & Education section has a learning center that covers courses, career management and development, and other training information.

Federation of State Boards of Physical Therapy
124 West St. S, Third Floor
Alexandria, VA 22314
www.fsbpt.org

Every state requires physical therapists to pass the examination administered by this organization before they can practice. The website covers basic information about becoming a physical therapist and provides details about taking the national exam.

Sports Statistician

What Does a Sports Statistician Do?

Keith Woolner is a professional sports statistician. He first fell in love with this field growing up in the 1980s. Woolner spent his time memorizing statistics on the back of baseball cards. Each player's batting average, number of hits, stolen bases, and other information are all compiled by sports statisticians. Woolner's fascination with sports statistics continued when he was a student at Massachusetts Institute of Technology, and his dream came true in 2007, when he was hired by the Cleveland Indians as a sports statistician. Woolner explains his job as director of baseball analytics, which involves organizing, analyzing, and presenting statistics. "We help baseball operations put the best possible team on the field," he says. "In many cases, that involves developing statistical models to measure player value, forecast future performance, and answer questions about game strategy and tactics."[14]

There are several types of statisticians. Woolner is an academic sports statistician; he analyzes data on players and game strategies and tactics.

He uses this information to search for trends and create forecasts that general managers can use to rack up more wins in the future.

Recorders are another type of sports statistician. This can be a dream job for a sports fan. Recorders are part of a crew that goes to sporting events and records statistics in real time. Recorders serve as official scorekeepers—they take down statistics as events happen, prepare midgame and final summary reports for the media, and draft up final stats for league records. Statistics crews are also called on to resolve disputed calls by umpires and referees.

Some sports statisticians are called bookies or bookmakers. Their job is illegal in every state except Nevada, where thousands of bookmakers earn huge salaries. Bookmakers study statistics to set odds on the outcome of sporting events. The odds accurately reflect how likely any particular outcome might be. As gambling expert Brad Johnson explains, bookmakers need to have a solid understanding of mathematical and statistical principles and be "very knowledgeable about the sports for which they are pricing markets; thus, they often specialize in just one or two."[15]

Working the Numbers

There is an old joke that suggests people become statisticians because they can't handle the excitement of accounting. But those who spend their days as sports statisticians can combine the less-than-exciting numbers work with their love of the game. Aleph Sample discovered this after he was hired by the Colorado Rockies in 2007. Sample was fresh out of college with a master's degree in statistics. At the time, professional sports teams were just beginning to use statisticians and the team manager did not quite know what to do with him. Sample spent most of his days sitting at a desk in an office eight blocks from Coors Field, where the team played.

Sample soon tired of sitting at a desk and began attending as many practices as possible. When the team traveled, Sample went with them, paying his own way. He kept detailed records about everything he saw, read, or heard about players, practices, games, and baseball trends. Sample filled a thick notebook with numbers, sticky notes, ticket stubs, and newspaper clippings. The team manager took notice and asked Sample to explain what he was doing. Sample showed the manager basic outcome data, like how many hits, walks, runs, errors, and home runs each player was responsible for. He presented charts that showed where each ball was hit on the field, what kinds of pitches were thrown, and various situations faced by each batter and pitcher. Using this information Sample developed measures of player value, forecasts of their future performances, and ways to improve game plans.

The manager quickly saw the value in the work. Sample was given permission to hire a team of analysts and programmers to support data-driven decision making. The statisticians developed scouting reports, coaching assessments, psychological profiles, and medical histories on every player. They compiled business records like player service time, contract data, and negotiation records.

How Do You Become a Sports Statistician?

It is not necessary to be a mathematics mastermind to become a sports statistician—but it helps. Those who work in the field are first and foremost statisticians who have at least a master's degree in statistics, mathematics, economics, or other quantitative field. Statisticians are educated in linear algebra, calculus, probability, statistical theory, and survey methodology. Many have degrees in related fields such as computer science, engineering, and physics.

According to Woolner, sports statisticians rely on three sets of skills. Quantitative skills rely on understanding statistics and math, which can be used to make sense of raw data. These skills can be developed in applied statistics courses, which cover subjects like regression methods, hypothesis testing, linear and logistic models, time series, data mining, machine learning, and charts, graphs, and other data visualizations.

Technical skills are also important to have, and they involve knowing how to use statistical software programs like R/S-PLUS, Stata, and Matlab. Sports statisticians also need to master advanced spreadsheet software so they can work with tables, charts, macros, and scripting. Statisticians need a deep understanding of how such software works so they can adjust it to their own purposes. "The more self-reliant you are at extracting and manipulating your data directly, the more quickly you can explore your data and test ideas," says Woolner. "So being adept with the technology you're likely to encounter will help tremendously."[16]

The third skill is domain knowledge, which refers to a comprehensive understanding of the subject being studied. For sports statisticians this means knowing every rule of the game, understanding how the front office operates, and how players are recruited and developed. Domain knowledge helps the statistician understand what information is available, how it is collected, and how it is used to solve problems. This part of the job can be fun; in fact, one way sports statisticians keep their domain knowledge current is by reading their favorite sports blogs and websites.

Internships

One way college students who major in statistics can advance their knowledge is to do an internship. Rebecca Nichols, the education outreach director of the American Statistical Association, explains the benefits of this experience. "Internships are a win-win for everybody involved. The student gets to work with practicing statisticians who are proficient in their fields and to learn what it is like to work in an industrial, laboratory, or office setting." Meanwhile, there are benefits to companies that hire or sponsor internships, too. "The organization providing the internship benefits from students' fresh ideas," says Nichols, "and receives the opportunity to evaluate the student's potential for future employment."[17]

Personality and Skills

Sports statisticians use statistics, calculus, and linear algebra every day. As such, they need strong mathematical and analytical skills to compile and analyze large amounts of data. Computer aptitude is necessary, especially for sports statisticians who write their own software programs to design and develop techniques and statistical models. Highly developed problem-solving skills are needed to overcome problems regarding data collection and analysis.

Statisticians also need to be able to communicate clearly. According to sports statistical analyst Keith Goldner: "The ability

Watching Sports for a Living

"I'm a huge sports fan and love watching sports for a living. I get to work in something I love, and my work can help a team win. Sometimes, I'll act as a consultant to a team, helping to come up with best plays, analyze player performance, and assess the dollar value of a player. With that information, the team can make decisions and may improve its chances of winning."

—Sports statistical analyst Keith Goldner

Quoted in Dennis Viloria, "Sports Statistical Analyst," Bureau of Labor Statistics, September 2015. www.bls.gov.

to communicate information effectively is the most important skill when dealing with anyone outside this field. You have to explain complex mathematical concepts and why they're important, sometimes face to face and other times through blog posts or articles."[18]

Career Advancement

Most sports statisticians begin their careers in government, finance, insurance, science, education, or health care. They compile sports statistics as a hobby or work as bloggers, writers, and advisers on a part-time basis. This can lead to landing full-time work with a professional sports team. Goldner describes how he moved his career forward.

> I knew that if I could create an opportunity for myself, I could prove my value. Whenever I attended a conference, I'd make a list of people I wanted to meet and offered to help with any extra work. That way, when a new job opened up, they'd think of me. . . . Then someone passed my name to a pro team that was starting a new analytics department, and I started there while still in school.[19]

Salary and Future Outlook

The amount of money a sports statistician can make varies greatly depending on their employment situation. According to the Bureau of Labor Statistics (BLS) the average wage for all statisticians in 2016 was $80,500. Salary surveys conducted by the website PayScale show the median pay for a sports statistician in 2016 was $70,500. Those on the high end of the pay scale earned over $110,000, while those on the lower end earned around $48,000. Bookmakers in Nevada can earn more than $200,000 annually.

The BLS says employment for all statisticians is expected to grow rapidly, 34 percent by 2024. This is due to the rise of what is called big data, the information generated by millions of people communicating and conducting business over the Internet. Companies compile this data and are increasingly relying on statisticians to interpret the numbers, which they use to predict future trends in buying, social behavior, and even voting.

While the BLS does not keep information about sports statisticians specifically, the entire field is expanding quickly. Ben Alamar, sports statistician for the Oklahoma City Thunder basketball team, says, "As decision makers gain more exposure to information that analysis can provide, they become more interested [in this work]. . . . The general concept of using statistics is gaining more acceptance; these factors will lead to more teams employing large analytics groups."[20]

Find Out More

American Statistics Association (ASA)
732 N. Washington St.
Alexandria, VA 22314
www.amstat.org

The ASA was founded in 1839 to support the development and application of statistical science. The association offers something for statistics students of all ages, including information about competitions, career advancement, and internships.

Association of Sports Analytics Professionals (ASAP)
www.sportsanalyticsprofessionals.com

ASAP is a professional organization dedicated to advancing the use of sports statistics. The association's website features educational blogs, career advice, and interesting "Stat of the Week" listings.

Digital Analytics Association (DAA)
401 Edgewater Pl., Suite 600
Wakefield, MA 01880
www.digitalanalyticsassociation.org

This organization is focused on analyzing Internet data and features blogs, job listings for statisticians, and research resources.

SAS

100 SAS Campus Dr.
Cary, NC 27513
www.sas.com

SAS, once known as Statistical Analysis Systems, focuses on using analytics to understand how professional sports teams win games. The website has free tutorials, an e-learning section, live web classes, and offers certification in various fields of statistics.

Sports Nutritionist

What Does a Sports Nutritionist Do?

Nutritionists recommend that an average twenty-eight-year-old male who works a desk job should consume about twenty-four hundred calories a day. Compare this to the average National Football League (NFL) quarterback, who needs to eat six thousand calories a day during football season! However, this does not mean football players live on donuts and pizza. Players eat a lot of food—six meals a day in season. But their diets are specially designed by a sports nutritionist, sometimes called a sports dietitian. These professionals create finely tuned dietary regimens for each player on a team. These diets differ depending on what a player needs. "Players who are in need of gaining size and strength, will be required to consume large amounts of protein and carbohydrates. These players can expect to consume a lot of chicken, eggs, beef, and pasta," says nutritionist and former NFL punter Steve Weatherford. "Meanwhile players who are in need of lowering their weights so that they can remain light on their feet, can expect to see a lot of fruits and vegetables."[21]

Sports nutritionists have in-depth knowledge of how food affects the body. They analyze each player's body type, training cycle, and performance goals to design nutrition programs that balance the intake of proteins, fats, carbohydrates, fluids, and dietary supplements. Sports nutritionists create a variety of diets for each athlete; some are intended to sustain an athlete during training, and others are intended to help an athlete perform at their best during the playing season.

Above all, nutritionists help athletes achieve and maintain desired levels of body mass, body fat, and muscle mass that are consistent with good health and performance. As a result, sports nutrition is becoming increasingly important to combating obesity in youth and collegiate athletics. According to Maria Breen, sports nutritionist at the University of Georgia (UGA), athletes need to consume a lot of calories in order to have enough energy to play. That said, there is a big difference between consuming calories and consuming the *right* calories. "If you're not taught how to eat as an athlete and you're just told you've got to gain weight so [you] eat all this food, you're likely contributing to some of the [health problems] that may develop later in life," says Breen. "We're that area of impact and change."[22]

Sports nutritionists help athletes work through eating disorders, food allergies, mineral deficiencies, and gastrointestinal problems. They evaluate nutritional supplements for safety, effectiveness, and quality. They also devise special diets that focus on recovery when players are injured. For example, healthy fats from avocados, nuts, and fish help the body defend against inflammation.

Athletes rely on their sports nutritionists to keep them performing their best and playing for as long as they can. Says Susan Kleiner, who works with the Seattle Seahawks, "Most of them understand that [good nutrition] will make a difference in their performance and even more probably understand it's going to make a difference in the length of their playing life. And that translates to dollars for them."[23]

Working as a Sports Nutritionist

Sports nutritionists' daily work can vary depending on the situation. Some design programs that cover every meal an athlete will eat on every day of the year. Others take a less rigorous approach. Sports nutritionist Kate Moran takes a very one-on-one approach to working with the baseball players of the Minnesota Twins. Her job is to help improve players' health, wellness, and performance. "I take a very education-centric approach, and really base what I do on the needs of the client," she says. "If they're looking for a meal plan that's really spelled out, I'll do that, or if they want to go to the grocery store together, I'll do that, too. It's about helping them improve skills individually to meet their goals."[24]

In addition to working with individuals, Moran leads educational seminars where she speaks to the entire team about food-related topics. She also consults with coaching staff and trainers about training, pregame, and postgame meals while working with caterers and other food preparation staff to ensure her dietary guidelines are followed.

Sports nutritionists who work on the collegiate level usually have a wider range of duties. For example, Breen oversees the nutritional needs of seven hundred UGA student athletes in twenty-one sports programs, including baseball, swimming, gymnastics, women's basketball, and cross country. Her job involves educating teams, one-on-one counseling, and writing four-week menu cycles for all lunches and dinners. One important aspect of Breen's job is writing team menus for away games: "If . . . their pre-meet meal is going to be in the hotel, I'm the one who writes all the menus for all their pre-meet meals because you can never know what the hotel is going to do and you can ask them to do anything—so I do! I write down exactly what they're going to be eating the night before and the morning of."[25]

How Do You Become a Sports Nutritionist?

Aspiring sports nutritionists need at least a bachelor's degree in nutrition or sports nutrition. However, one likely needs a master's degree in nutrition or exercise physiology to work for a college or professional sports team. Many sports nutritionists must also obtain a state license and a professional certification. State license requirements vary from state to state.

It can take six to twelve months to get certified as a Registered Dietitian Nutritionist (RDN), which involves getting supervised, practical, hands-on experience in sports training or nutrition. An RDN can be obtained from an accredited dietetic internship program. There are four types of programs, and each requires a minimum of twelve hundred hours of participation. Programs typically pair students with mentors who work in clinical and community nutrition and food service management.

RDN certification is obtained from the Accreditation Council for Education in Nutrition and Dietetics (ACEND), which is part of the Academy of Nutrition and Dietetics. Those who pass the ACEND exam can call themselves an RDN. The council requires RDNs to get seventy-five hours of continuing education credit hours every five years to maintain certification.

RDNs often obtain further certification through the National Association of Sports Nutrition. This organization offers a Licensed Primary Sports Nutritionist credential to those who have experience as certified practitioners. The course requires applicants to attend a nutrition seminar, complete a home study course, and pass an examination.

Personality and Skills

A successful sports nutritionist combines the skills of an educator, a health care professional, and an athletic trainer. All of these professions require compassion and excellent communication, as well as analytical and problem-solving skills. Sports nutritionists need to be able to discuss complex dietary topics in ways players can understand. They should be comfortable working in individual and group settings. The ability to listen is also important, as sports nutritionists must tailor their programs to individual athletes' needs and feedback.

Sports nutritionists need good research skills to stay up-to-date on the latest food, sports, and nutritional information. They also need to continuously update their knowledge so they can maintain their certifications. Sports nutritionists use their problem-solving abilities nearly every day when they evaluate the needs and concerns of their clients and help them manage their performance and health. Creative thinking is useful when formulating diverse programs that address the needs of individual athletes.

Who Is Hiring Sports Nutritionists?

Sports nutrition has become an important component of collegiate, professional, and Olympic sports teams. Sports nutritionists work for colleges and universities, amateur and professional sports teams, recreation and fitness facilities, gyms, and health care associations.

Some sports nutritionists work in community and public health settings, advising the public on ways to improve their quality of life through healthy eating habits. They teach in classrooms where they instruct students and others on the science of foods and nutrition. Sports nutritionists also work in the research and development departments of food and pharmaceutical companies, where they might conduct experiments to develop new foods and medicines. Some sports nutritionists are self-employed and work as consultants. They visit clients in their homes, visit grocery stores, and work in kitchens with chefs and other food preparation staff.

Helping Clients Perform and Feel Better

"Having already high-performing clients feel better, perform better and improve their health, while having them tell you it has changed their life is very rewarding. To be able to take science, and apply it practically to different lifestyles and needs, with a balance of challenging and understanding each person, is a great achievement. . . . The most exciting part to me is when my athletes and my clients are able to develop skills around nutrition and apply it to their lifestyle."

—Meg Mangano, sports nutritionist for the Los Angeles Clippers

Quoted in Medina Parilla, "Women's History Month Interview Series: Q&A with Sports Nutritionist Meg Mangano," Double G Sports, March 19, 2015. http://doublegsports.com.

Career Advancement

Many sports nutritionists begin their careers teaching at the college level and move on to full- or part-time jobs in a school's athletic department. Nutritionists can advance their careers by joining professional organizations such as the Academy of Nutrition and Dietetics, the International Society of Sports Nutrition, and Sports, Cardiovascular and Wellness Nutrition. These organizations offer seminars, career tips, and networking opportunities to nutritionists in all phases of a career.

What Is the Future Outlook for Sports Nutritionists?

According to the Bureau of Labor Statistics (BLS), opportunities for all nutritionists are expected to grow by 16 percent by 2024. The field is expanding because athletes and trainers, as well as the general public, are increasingly emphasizing the importance of health, nutrition, and exercise. Sports nutrition is a new field; it was not universally recognized until the early twenty-first century, and many teams did not employ a full-time nutritionist until recently. "[Just a few years ago] many student-athletes weren't thinking about how they should eat for performance or they weren't doing it right," says Breen. "Fast forward a few years and every athlete knows who their sports nutritionist is."[26] This shift is evident in professional sports; Major League Baseball and the Major League Baseball Players Association made it mandatory for all teams to employ a sports nutritionist in 2016.

While the average annual salary for all nutritionists was $58,920 in 2016, nutritionists who work in college or professional sports can earn more than $82,410, according to the BLS.

Find Out More

Academy of Nutrition and Dietetics
120 S. Riverside Plaza, Suite 2190
Chicago, IL 60606
www.eatrightpro.org

The Academy of Nutrition and Dietetics offers a certification program through its Commission on Dietetic Registration that provides a Registered Dietitian Nutritionist credential. The organization's website provides career development advice, professional development tools, and other student resources.

Collegiate and Professional Sports Dietitians Association
8193 Grey Fox Dr.
West Chester, OH 45069
www.sportsrd.org

This association of professional dietitians offers student memberships to those in undergraduate or graduate dietetics programs and to those pursuing an allied health care field related to athletics or nutrition. The group provides sports-specific fact sheets with the most current nutrition-related research into practical eating and recovery strategies.

National Association of Sports Nutrition
8898 Clairemont Mesa Blvd., Suite J
San Diego, CA 92123
http://nasnutrition.com

This nationally recognized organization provides licenses and certifications for sports nutritionists and offers online videos, articles, and educational materials for students.

Sports, Cardiovascular, and Wellness Nutrition
230 Washington Ave. Ext., Suite 101
Albany, NY 12203
www.scandpg.org

This group is for registered dietitians with expertise in sports, physical activity, and wellness. Student members are an important part of the organization and the website offers career tips, internship advice, and online educational resources.

Sporting Event Planner

A Few Facts

Median Salary
$47,350 a year in 2016

Minimum Educational Requirements
Bachelor's degree in hospitality management

Personal Qualities
Highly organized, good communicator, can perform multiple tasks at once

Working Conditions
Indoors in offices, hotels, restaurants, and convention centers; local and national travel is often required; long irregular hours including evenings, weekends, and holidays

Number of Jobs
100,000 in 2015

Job Outlook
Expected to grow 10 percent by 2024

What Does a Sporting Event Planner Do?

Mike Duhon began working for the National Cheerleaders Association in 2011. In 2016 he was in charge of planning the group's College Nationals competition in Daytona Beach, Florida. The event attracted more than sixty-six hundred cheerleaders who performed perfect backflips and launched teammates twenty feet into the air. While Duhon cannot jump or tumble, he is extremely coordinated when it comes to planning sporting events. Duhon is a master of contracts, budgeting, event registration forms, and scheduling. He excels in negotiating with venues and hotels and earns cheers from staff, judges, and caterers. Duhon also works to meet the needs of television crews. "I make sure the backdrop and lighting is what they need, and I make sure they have all the power they need for the show,"[27] he says. While the 2016 competition only lasted five days, it was the result of eight months of planning on Duhon's part.

Duhon's duties are typical for anyone who works as a sporting event planner. These people work for individual sports teams, public stadium authorities, or private corporations like the National Football League (NFL) or Major League Baseball (MLB). Sporting event planners also work with nonprofit groups like charities and advocacy organizations. They specialize in banquets and sports charity events that raise money for various causes.

Working as a Sporting Event Planner

From professional tennis matches to the Super Bowl to the Olympics, sporting event planners are at the center of the action. Sporting event planners work with teams and associated organizations to arrange every aspect of an event. Sporting event planners constantly interact with the public. They consult with clients to determine the time, place, theme, audience size, and cost of an event. They search for meeting sites such as convention centers and hotels and determine the quality of nearby lodging and services. They consider logistics like how easy it is to get to and from an event and nearby attractions that might interest visitors.

Planners contract with vendors who provide food, decorations, audio and visual equipment, and other necessities. They hire entertainers, bands, speakers, and interpreters and coordinate activities like guest registration. Sporting event planners work with caterers, waitstaff, and bartenders to ensure smooth and efficient food preparation and service. When the event is over, planners pay vendors, coordinate cleanup, and meet with clients to obtain feedback.

The work requires a highly organized mind and nerves of steel, as a lot can go wrong. "I have never had complete confidence about an event prior to completion," says Duhon. "Regardless of preparation, there are always external factors that have the potential to steer an event in the wrong direction."[28]

How Do You Become a Sporting Event Planner?

In the past, many event planners did not have special training. They were people who were involved in other aspects of the

Making Decisions on the Fly

"You're going to incur challenges at every event—some small, some big, some more daunting than others. As a planner, you have to be willing to make decisions on the fly and roll with what's given to you. Issues like, [in 2013] in Daytona, the weather. That's an outside venue and we've never had an issue with weather, but . . . it rained. . . . [We] had to reconfigure the entire competition to move it inside two days before the event occurred. It's an issue not only with our customers but TV production and sponsors, our staff, our attendees."

—Mike Duhon, event planner for National Cheerleaders Association

Quoted in Libby Hoppe, "Q&A: Mike Duhon, National Cheerleaders Association," Connect Sports, June 18, 2013. www.connectsports.com.

sports or convention business who worked as assistants and took charge of planning events. However, the nature of sporting event planning has become more complex in recent years. Employers now prefer candidates who have a bachelor's degree in sports management or hospitality management. Coursework for these degrees is varied and includes subjects such as hotel management, meeting and event management, marketing, public relations, food production, cost control and analysis, and business communications. Sporting event planner applicants who do not have a bachelor's degree are expected to have at least two years of experience working in the field.

Certification and Licensing

Sporting event planners who obtain certification have an easier time finding a job and a better chance at advancing to higher career levels. Certification is voluntary and available in several specialized fields. A Certified Meeting Professional credential from the Events Industry Council (EIC) is available to convention, meeting, and exhibition planners. The EIC certification requires applicants to prove they have had three years of experience and recent employment in the industry. They must also pass a written exam that covers various functions of event planning.

Volunteer Work and Internships

Many prospective sporting event planners gain vital experience offering their time and services for free. Local charities are always looking for volunteers to help plan fund-raisers, charity runs, and other sports-related events. Students can also volunteer to plan fund-raisers and banquets for sports teams.

Personality and Skills

Successful sporting event planners are perfectionists. They often deal with powerful clients—and even celebrity athletes—who expect every aspect of an event to be excellent. Sporting event planners must also be skilled multitaskers. At any given moment they are juggling problems and requests from a number of clients, guests, and vendors.

Good communication skills are required since sporting event planners often find themselves giving orders to many people at once, in person, on the phone, and via text message and e-mail. Organizational skills are also important; efficient people react calmly when the pressure is on and make good decisions when clients, workers, and vendors are stressing out. According to fund-raising event planner Anne Siegel, this requires the ability to delegate responsibility and to know when to rely on others. "You have to go to other people for help," she says. "I'm savvy enough now that I've learned I can't be the be-all, end-all for everything. When you're so thick and deep in the details, it's easy to overlook something. I take those opportunities to have checks and balances with the staff."[29]

Coordinating sporting events requires planners to work long hours. Nicola Briggs, who has planned numerous sporting events, believes her success hinges on loving what she does. "You need to be passionate about every particular job you are doing and every client you are working for," she says. "You need to be prepared to work hard and sometimes very long hours throughout the year. It is not a simple 9-5/Monday-Friday job. However if you put the hard work in it can be very rewarding."[30]

A creative mind is another asset for successful sporting event planners. No two projects are entirely the same, and challenging problems often require imaginative solutions. Planners who put on annual events need to make sure they improve the event and make it even more fun than it was the year before. This takes resourcefulness and creativity. As Siegel says, "If we've done it before, I don't want to do it again. . . . How can we elevate this event next time? How can we make it better? That excites me."[31]

Perhaps the most important trait a sporting event planner can have is modesty. People who make a career in this field work behind the scenes to create perfect events for the pleasure of others. Planners are not at the party to enjoy themselves. As Siegel

First to Arrive, Last to Leave

"Be prepared to work some pretty unorthodox hours. You'll usually be the first to arrive at a venue and the last to leave. . . . However, this flexibility is also what makes becoming an event planner so exciting; you essentially run your own show. From arranging site visits to negotiating with vendors, coordinating an event is all up to you—which means you plan your schedule. Not to mention, many event planners travel a lot. A flexible, jet-setting career isn't just a dream for event planners, but it does take some exceptional time-management skills."

—Alison Kasko, event planner

Alison Kasko, "What They Didn't Tell You About Becoming an Event Planner," *Pointers for Planners* (blog), November 1, 2016. https://blog.qceventplanning.com.

says: "You can't think it's all about you."[32] Usually, the only time a sporting event planner gets a lot of attention is when something goes wrong. When everything unfolds perfectly, few people will stop to thank or even notice the person who spent months organizing the event.

Working Conditions

Planning sporting events is definitely not a desk job. While sporting event planners do use an office as a base of operations, they are often on the move. They attend meetings with clients, vendors, and other personnel. Some even travel to distant cities and exotic locations to inspect convention centers, restaurants, and other venues. "Event planners travel a lot," says event planner Alison Kasko. "A flexible, jet-setting career isn't just a dream for event planners."[33]

Who's Hiring?

In 2015 there were about one hundred thousand event planning positions. Most event planners work for private companies in the business sector. Sporting event planners are hired by companies like IMG and the Anschutz Entertainment Group. Events such as the Super Bowl, the Fiesta Bowl, the Senior PGA Championship, and the NCAA Division I Men's Basketball Tournament hire sporting event managers as staff members.

Most event planners work for private companies across a wide range of industries. About 20 percent specialize in planning for professional, civic, or sports organizations. About 15 percent plan events for the lodging and food service industry. Around 10 percent of event planners are self-employed.

Career Advancement

Some sporting event planners start out as administrative assistants to executive directors, marketing directors, public relations directors, sales managers, directors of operations, and client services coordinators. In this role, they usually work on small or individual pieces of work related to an event, such as booking travel arrangements or lodging for out-of-town guests. A sporting event planner might start out as a conference coordinator and move up to a higher-paying position, such as a meeting manager or executive director of sporting event planning. Some sporting event planners get into the business as caterers or managers of a hotel or restaurant. Others move from event planning to start their own companies or become self-employed consultants.

Those who have experience coordinating sporting events can also break into other aspects of the sports industry. The job can lead to higher-paying careers in public relations, sports media sales, facility management, or event marketing.

What Is the Future Outlook for Sporting Event Planners?

According to the Bureau of Labor Statistics (BLS), the number of people working as event planners is expected to grow by 10 percent through 2024. The largest states—California, New York, Texas, and Florida—have the greatest number of event planners. The BLS lists the average salary for all event planners as $47,350 in 2016, but compensation levels vary depending on the level of responsibility, length of service, education, location, and type of organization for which one works. For example, sporting event planners on the college level can expect to earn $25,000 to $60,000, according to SportsCareerFinder. Planners for the NFL can expect salaries in the $43,000 to $79,000 range.

Find Out More

Events Industry Council (EIC)
700 N. Fairfax St., Suite 510
Alexandria, VA 22314
www.eventscouncil.org

The EIC is the leading organization for the meetings, conventions, and exhibition industry. The website provides access to the Certified Meeting Professional (CMP) industry certification program. The CMP Career Center features sample interview questions, job descriptions, job listings, and information about hiring.

National Association of Collegiate Directors of Athletics (NACDA)
www.nacda.com

The NACDA is a large association of collegiate athletics administrators. The organization has two student training institutes: Management/Leadership and Sports Management. The association's intern program is aimed at students who aspire to collegiate athletics administration.

North American Society for Sport Management (NASSM)
135 Winterwood Dr.
Butler, PA 16001
www.nassm.com

The group is made up of professionals and students involved in supporting and encouraging study, research, scholarly writing, and professional development in all areas of sport management including event planning. The organization includes a student board that organizes events at the annual NASSM conference, where student attendees can network with practicing sport managers and professors.

Professional Convention Management Association (PCMA)
35 E. Wacker Dr., Suite 500
Chicago, IL 60601
www.pcma.org

The PCMA specializes in education, networking, and community engagement organization for planners of meetings, conventions, and business events. The organization sponsors an education foundation that funds grants, scholarships, and research programs. The site also features job listings.

Umpire/Referee

A Few Facts

Median Salary
$24,840 in 2016

Minimum Educational Requirements
High school diploma

Personal Qualities
Athletic ability, good vision, in-depth knowledge of a game's rules, calm under pressure

Working Conditions
Indoors or outdoors in all sorts of weather; irregular hours, including part time, evenings, weekends, and holidays

Number of Jobs
19,800 in 2014

Job Outlook
Demand expected to increase 20 percent by 2020

What Does an Umpire/Referee Do?

Almost every sports fan has screamed at the TV when an umpire or referee makes a call against their team. But those sports officials are simply enforcing the numerous complex rules that govern every sport. Without umpires and referees, most games would descend into chaos.

Umpires and referees officiate at sports events and make sure everyone plays fairly. They signal when rules are broken and assess penalties when necessary. Umpires and referees act as judges, settling the claims and complaints of players and coaches. In addition to making calls, umpires and referees have the option of removing players and coaches who are argumentative or hostile. Umpires and referees can even have abusive or unruly fans kicked out of the stadium.

Whether a person is called an umpire or referee depends on the sport. In baseball and softball, two to six umpires are charged with officiating a game. An umpire in chief, or home plate umpire, calls balls and strikes, foul balls, fair balls, and makes calls about batters

A referee blows his whistle to halt play. Umpires and referees officiate at sporting events. They make sure everyone plays fairly, signal when rules are broken, and assess penalties when necessary.

and base runners. Other umpires are called base umpires, as they are stationed near first, second, and third base. During professional championship games two more umpires will officiate, and they are stationed in right field and left field.

Sports officials who oversee hockey, soccer, and boxing are known as referees. Three referees officiate at basketball games; the head referee is called the crew chief. During collegiate and professional football games seven officials operate on the field. They are all usually called referees, but this is incorrect. Each official has a specific duty, and each position has its own name: referee, umpire, head linesman, line judge, back judge, side judge, and center judge. In tennis, one official called an umpire works on the court, and one official called a referee works off the court.

Working on the Court and Field

The daily work of an umpire or referee depends on the sport. Basketball referees are known to work the hardest. The rules are complex and the speed of play is very fast. The work of baseball umpires is much less physically demanding. Major League Baseball (MLB) umpire Adam Hamari describes his typical day: "Get up, play golf, eat lunch, take a nap and head to the ballpark about an hour before game time. . . . Once we get to the ballpark, we might discuss plays that have happened or other intricacies of the series. Some ballparks have weird ground rules or other things of the sort that we might talk about."[34]

Professional football officials spend a great deal of time keeping up with the rules of the game. National Football League (NFL) referee Ed Hochuli describes his work life: "Each official has to take a written test every week during the season and every month in the offseason. I personally spent an hour a day studying rules. Rules in the NFL are extremely complicated. Rules enforcement in the NFL is extremely complicated. We have a case book that has 1,000 plays. I find in order to stay on top of the rules, I read them all the time."[35]

How Do You Become an Umpire/Referee?

A college degree is not necessary to pursue a career as an umpire or referee. Many officials began umpiring and refereeing in high school or even middle school. Some start out as athletes who are familiar with the rules of the game. Whatever one's previous experience, anyone officiating a game needs in-depth knowledge of the rules and regulations that govern the sport. Every prospective umpire and referee needs to purchase a rule book and study rules online.

Professional baseball umpires must know every aspect of the Official Baseball Rules, which is published in book form and on the MLB website. Some of the rules have remained unchanged since the 1800s, while others have been updated over the years by the nine-member Playing Rules Committee. The committee meets once a year to discuss possible rule changes submitted by umpires, players, baseball executives, and even fans. Like an accountant who is required to study new tax laws every year,

Stepping into the Big Leagues

"I don't think that there is anything that can actually prepare you for the Major Leagues. Stepping on to a big-league field is so much different than any other assignment that I've ever worked. The lights are brighter, the stadium is bigger and the stage is larger. You work your entire career for the opportunity to have that happen, and you prepare yourself both physically and mentally for that challenge so when you do get the chance, you're as prepared as you can be."

—Adam Hamari, Major League Baseball umpire

Quoted in "Q&A: Major League Baseball Umpire, Marquette Native Adam Hamari," *Mining Journal*, May 3, 2017. www.miningjournal.net.

an umpire must remain up-to-date on every rule change implemented each year by the Playing Rules Committee.

While experience is essential, those who wish to officiate at the collegiate and professional level can benefit from continuing education. For example, Hamari started umpiring Little League games when he was twelve years old. When he went to college he umpired college games. After graduating in 2006 Hamari attended the Jim Evans Academy of Professional Umpiring in Colorado. This school offers a five-week professional course with classroom and field instruction.

Those who dream of becoming a National Basketball Association (NBA) referee can participate in the official league recruitment process. Prospective referees can visit the NBA Officiating Opportunities website, which maps out the process. Candidates can attend national tryouts or National Collegiate Athletic Association camps, or get involved through an NBA, high school, or college organization. The top one hundred candidates are evaluated by the NBA Referee Scouting Group. Winners are trained at elite camps and put to work at Summer League games. Those who excel can eventually work in the NBA and Women's National Basketball Association (WNBA).

Personality and Skills

A sports official needs many of the skills and personality traits found in a good athlete or coach. Umpires and referees have to be team players, as they usually officiate games with a number of other sports officials. A healthy body weight and a degree of athletic ability is also important. Officials are required to run, walk, stand, and squat for hours at a time.

Officials need to be in good physical condition so that they can get out of a player's way very quickly. While staying out of the way, umpires and referees need to quickly position themselves where they can see the play, make calls, and determine the outcome. Taking it easy is not an option when the outcome of a game depends on split-second decisions made by officials. NBA crew chief Bob Delaney knows this firsthand. "We're running up and down the floor with the greatest athletes in the world," he says. "In order to keep up with them, we know that we have to be in the best physical condition we can achieve, because we know that if we are physically tired it will lead to poor decision-making."[36]

Although sports fans often accuse umpires and referees of being blind, good vision is a requirement of the job. In sports like diving and gymnastics, officials are also expected to clearly observe an athlete's form and body movements.

Working Conditions

Umpires and referees work indoors and outdoors, depending on the sport. Football officials often work in rain, snow, and frigid temperatures. Hockey referees spend hours on the ice. Whatever the sport, the job typically requires a great deal of travel. For many officials this involves long bus rides and overnight stays in cheap motels. Professional sports officials travel by air. Officiating games can also be very stressful; athletes, coaches, and fans can become verbally and even physically abusive and there is a great deal of pressure to make correct calls.

Who's Hiring?

While most umpires and referees involved in youth sports are volunteers, sports officials can earn a paycheck working for high schools, colleges, and professional leagues. Like many other aspects of employment, the Internet has changed the way referees get hired. Websites like Rent-A-Ref connect leagues, teams, and coaches to referees who have been interviewed, screened, and prequalified to match the skill level of the players. The website notifies referees when there are games in the area and takes care of issuing payments, taking a small percentage of each transaction.

Career Advancement

Umpires and referees often follow the same career path as athletes. They start as volunteers in youth athletics and move into collegiate sports or the minor leagues. Some eventually make it into the pros. Many umpires and referees, even those in professional sports, are part-time workers. For example, the NFL season only lasts about half a year and most officiating crews have long held jobs outside of football. Walt Coleman, a well-known referee, is a dairy farmer, while Hochuli is a lawyer. In 2017 the NFL announced it would hire seventeen game officials as full-time employees, but the league will continue to employ around four times that number as part-time officials.

Those who make it into professional sports can earn a good living, though pay varies drastically depending on the sport and how much one works. The Bureau of Labor Statistics (BLS) says that in 2014 around 19,800 people worked as umpires, referees, and other sports officials for a median salary of $25,660. In the beginning of their careers, NFL referees can earn around $70,000 annually, while the highest-paid referees pulled in $173,000 in 2017. Pay was expected to rise to $201,000 by 2019.

NBA referees work full time during the eight-month season, wherein each team plays eighty-two games. Depending on experience, an NBA referee earned from $150,000 to $550,000 annually in 2016. Umpires who work in the MLB get around $120,000 when they start out; senior umpires can earn upward of $300,000.

What Is the Future Outlook for Umpires and Referees?

The BLS predicts the number of umpire and referee jobs will increase 5 percent before 2024. However, the BLS figures do not take into account the increasing demand for sports officials at the high school and collegiate level. Low pay combined with long hours and abuse from fans has caused a referee shortage in several states. This has prompted recruiters from the National Association of Intercollegiate Athletics to visit college campuses in search of young basketball referees. As Kansas fitness coach Eli Egger explains: "I think that referees are very underrated and it is important that people who are passionate learn because it is . . . an important business."[37]

Keep Your Cool

"Referees work to keep the peace and make sure the game is played fairly. Obviously, on each side of the ball you have passionate people who at times let their emotions get the best of them. . . . It is very important to keep your cool. The players, coaches and fans can and should be fired up, excited, super passionate about trying to win. An official, on the other hand, has to remain cool and calm and see the game for what it is. . . . My job is to focus on the play at hand and get the play right."

—Evon Burroughs, NCAA college basketball referee

Quoted in "Q&A with NCAA College Basketball Referee & Boston Police Officer Evon Burroughs," BPD News, March 21, 2014. http://bpdnews.com.

Find Out More

Jim Evans Academy of Professional Umpiring

200 S. Wilcox St., #508
Castle Rock, CO 80104
www.umpireacademy.com

Many professional umpires have attended this school. Students interested in a career umpiring baseball will find information about onsite training, umpiring clinics, and scholarships.

National Association of Sports Officials (NASO)

2017 Lathrop Ave.
Racine, WI 53405
www.naso.org

The NASO provides members with a variety of educational resources, information, publications, and advice. The group's website instructs students on ways they can become officials in baseball, basketball, football, soccer, softball, and volleyball.

NBA Officiating Opportunities

https://nbaofficials.com

The NBA recruits referees from across the globe. This website provides a career map for students who wish to become professional NBA and WNBA officials.

Women Officiating Now (WON)

http://operations.nfl.com/the-officials/officiating-development/women-officiating-now-won

WON hosts clinics where women learn the basics of football and the fundamentals of officiating. The clinics are open to all women, no matter their background or skill level.

Sports Speech Therapist

A Few Facts

Median Salary

$74,680 a year in 2016

Minimum Educational Requirements

Master's degree

Personal Qualities

Analytical and communication skills, critical thinking, attention to detail, good listening skills, compassion

Working Conditions

Full-time work indoors in clinical settings

Number of Jobs

135,400 for all speech therapists in 2014

Job Outlook

21 percent growth before 2024 for all speech therapists

What Does a Sports Speech Therapist Do?

In 2007 Darren Sproles of the San Diego Chargers made football history by returning a kickoff and a punt for his first two National Football League (NFL) touchdowns in the same game. While Sproles's work on the field made him famous among football fans, he was honored by sports speech therapists—and those with speech impediments—when he helped celebrate National Stuttering Awareness Week in 2008. Sproles is one of many famous athletes who stutter. Other stutterers include basketball greats Bill Walton, Kenyon Martin, Bob Love, and professional golfer Ken Venturi.

Sproles began stuttering in first grade, but his speech impediment was not a real problem until he became a star football player at Kansas State University. "I had to talk to the media a lot, and once they put a camera in my face that's when it got bad,"[38] he says. While in college Sproles worked on his stuttering problem with speech-language pathologists (SLPs), medical professionals also known as speech therapists. He overcame his stuttering by learning to speak slower. His therapist taught him breathing exercises, which helped reduce his anxiety. He also spent hours reading books out loud to practice smooth speech. He stayed fluent by attending follow-up maintenance sessions with speech therapists. The therapy helped Sproles so much that he turned down the offer of an NFL contract in his junior year. Instead he worked to obtain a master's degree in speech-language pathology before joining the NFL upon graduation.

Those who make a career as a speech therapist often work to help people who stutter or lisp. However, the scope of the work is much broader. Speech therapists are highly educated health care professionals who use their understanding of anatomy, linguistics, genetics, and psychology to diagnose, treat, and prevent a wide range of disorders involving speech, communication, swallowing, and breathing. They evaluate a patient's problems, identify treatment options, carry out individualized treatment, and teach patients how to make sounds, improve their voice, and strengthen muscles used in swallowing. Speech therapists also help patients cope with their disorders.

Speech therapists help patients build their articulation skills, which include the physical ability to move the tongue, lips, and jaw to produce sounds. Those who stutter are evaluated for possible psychological and emotional problems related to anxiety and stress. Speech therapists work with people who have voice and resonance disorders caused by problems with their vocal cords and nasal and oral cavities. They treat cognitive-communication problems, which are difficulties in self-expression that are associated with brain functions like attention, memory, and reasoning.

Sports speech therapists work with athletes who have speech impediments or lack the communication skills necessary to give the interviews and speeches that are part of their high-profile job. Sports speech therapists also treat athletes who have suffered concussions, which can cause people to slur their words and have other speech problems. These speech therapists specialize in what is called cognitive rehabilitation, which involves helping injured athletes recover from brain injuries and helping them deal with communication difficulties. As sports speech therapist Jim D. Moss writes, "Many patients have expressed to me how helpful speech therapy has been for their recovery from the devastating effects of concussion."[39]

In recent years SLPs have been hired to treat athletes who suffer from a condition called vocal cord dysfunction (VCD). This is a type of respiratory disorder that interrupts the normal breathing cycle and causes shortness of breath, which can inhibit an athlete's performance or even cause them to faint on the field. Speech therapist Amika Osumi describes the condition: "The proper way for the body to breathe involves the vocal cords opening when inhaling and moving to a closed position when exhaling. But for someone with VCD, the opposite occurs: their vocal cords close when inhaling and can cause panic and exhaustion for an athlete."[40]

VCD is often misdiagnosed as asthma because the symptoms are similar, tightness in the throat during intense exercise accompanied by a high-pitched, abnormal wheezing sound known as stridor. In 2013 researchers discovered that VCD affected around 5 percent of adult athletes. Sports speech therapists are trained to recognize the symptoms of VCD and teach athletes relaxation techniques and breathing exercises that have been clinically proven to reduce symptoms.

Working as a Sports Speech Therapist

Sports speech therapists often work as part of a team that might include physicians, nurses, psychologists, and athletic trainers. When not treating patients, sports speech therapists spend a lot of time writing. They review and edit notes from sessions with clients, update detailed records of evaluations and patient progress, and file paperwork. Sports speech therapists often become professionally close to their clients. They help them celebrate successes and offer counseling during setbacks.

Speech therapist Anthony Salvatore works with young athletes within his local community to prevent serious injuries. Salvatore set up a concussion management clinic at the University of Texas at El

Paso to provide services to concussion patients and to help reduce traumatic brain injury (TBI) among student athletes. After establishing the program Salvatore reached out to athletics departments at middle schools and high schools to launch programs that allow student athletes to take courses on how to prevent concussions. They spend around thirty hours in a clinic that treats and tracks athletes with TBI. Salvatore also reviewed all community athletics programs for contact sports to make sure student athletes, some as young as six years old, were adequately protected. According to Salvatore: "I talked about a number of options on how to improve the safety of these kids. Data are just beginning to get collected, so we needed to be really conservative—especially with young children."[41] Salvatore also enlisted school-based speech therapists to enact changes in sports behavior.

How Do You Become a Sports Speech Therapist?

Anyone who wishes to work as a sports speech therapist needs at least a master's degree in speech-language pathology. Students who take an SLP master's degree program learn about topics such as voice articulation, literacy, neurological processes, and phonology, which covers the relationships among sounds that make up the basic components of a language. Classes are also conducted in clinical settings where students learn to diagnose and treat patients from different socioeconomic and linguistic backgrounds. Some students work to become fluent in other languages—those who are bilingual have better career opportunities.

Obtaining a master's in speech-language pathology is very demanding and requires great dedication. "It's a combination of science and language arts," says Kimberly O. Scanlon, who says prospective SLPs should have strong written and oral communication skills, as well as solid analytical skills. "If you are not interested in neurology, human development, or grammar, then it will be challenging to finish a program. In addition to needing a degree of natural aptitude, dedication, time, and research are required. Spending time in the library or clinic is a must if you want to graduate."[42]

Working with Trainers and Athletes

"Speech-language pathologists treating cases of [vocal cord dysfunction] in our speech clinic now seek the feedback and expertise of the [athletic trainer] who works directly with the athlete receiving services. . . . We have collaborated on cases involving athletes from soccer, track and field, basketball, swimming and crew. We have presented a regional speech-language conference and published a series of case narratives that highlight collaboration. . . . We have seen an increased awareness among our athletic training and speech-language pathology students who have learned through this interprofessional collaboration."

—Mary Pitti, sports speech-language pathologist

Mary Pitti and Michael Matheny, "Odd Couple? Or Dynamic Duo?," ASHA Leader, June 1, 2016. http://leader.pubs.asha.org.

After obtaining a degree graduate students participate in clinical fellowships. During these thirty-six-week fellowship programs graduates work full time with mentors to gain professional experience. Eighty percent of the time is spent assessing patients and making diagnoses, and screening, treating, and counseling clients.

After completing the clinical fellowship, speech therapists must obtain a Certificate of Clinical Competence in Speech-Language Pathology (CCC-SLP). This is issued by the Council on Academic Accreditation, which is part of the American Speech-Language-Hearing Association. Most employers require this certification. Every state requires speech therapists to be licensed, and obtaining a CCC-SLP satisfies some or all of the requirements for licensure. Speech therapists who work in schools often need teaching certificates.

Personality and Skills

Like other health care professionals, sports speech therapists need to have a great deal of compassion. They often work with athletes who need emotional support to deal with the frustration that accompanies their disorders. Communication skills are vital, since sports speech therapists need to clearly explain test results, propose treatments, and conduct therapeutic exercises. Sports speech therapists also need to be good listeners so they can understand a patient's symptoms and concerns. Good critical-thinking and analytical skills help sports speech therapists select proper diagnostic tools and adjust a patient's treatment plans.

Working Conditions

Sports speech therapists work in a variety of settings including schools, clinics, health care facilities, and in private practice. They might also work with athletes at training facilities and sports venues. Most work forty hours per week, but those who contract with sports teams might spend a substantial amount of time traveling.

Who's Hiring?

Around 40 percent of speech therapists worked at state, local, and private schools in 2014. Most others worked in clinics, hospitals, and other health care facilities. Around 5 percent worked directly for college and professional sports teams.

Career Advancement

Most speech therapists who work in sports start out as general SLPs. School-based SLPs often work with the athletic department where they can gain enough experience to move into the field of sports speech therapy full time. Others advance their careers by working at athletic clinics, where they can make contacts that allow them to open a private sports speech therapy practice.

What Is the Future Outlook for Sports Speech Therapists?

The Bureau of Labor Statistics (BLS) does not specifically track SLPs who work with athletes. According to the BLS, the median pay for all speech therapists in 2016 was $74,680. The BLS said the opportunities for SLPs will grow 21 percent before 2024. The predicted growth is based on an increased awareness of speech and language disorders in young children. This awareness has spurred the development of supportive programs and services, which is expected to lead to a need for more speech pathologists.

Find Out More

American Academy of Private Practice in Speech Pathology and Audiology (AAPPSPA)
www.aappspa.org

The AAPPSPA provides information, education, and support for its members. Prospective SLPs can learn about the business of professional speech-language pathology and learn details about working with children and adults in home offices, medical practices, hospitals, and schools and universities.

American College of Sports Medicine
401 W. Michigan St.
Indianapolis, IN 46202
www.acsm.org

This association represents students and professionals involved in seventy occupations within the sports medicine field, including SLPs. The website's Student Corner offers career resources, awards, a newsletter, and other information for those planning to make a career in sports medicine.

American Speech-Language-Hearing Association
2200 Research Blvd.
Rockville, MD 20850
www.asha.org

This organization is a professional, scientific, and credentialing institution for SLPs and students. The site offers information concerning careers, research, and continuing education. The affiliated Council on Academic Accreditation accredits education programs in speech-language pathology.

National Student Speech Language Hearing Association (NSSLHA)
2200 Research Blvd.
Rockville, MD 20850
www.asha.org

The NSSLHA has chapters at more than 325 colleges and universities. Membership is open to graduate or undergraduate students interested in speech-language pathology. The group's website features publications and information about leadership and certification programs.

SOURCE NOTES

Introduction: An Industry-Wide Hiring Binge

1. Jason Belzer, "Want a Job in the Sports Industry? Good News, Because It's an Employee's Market," *Forbes*, December 17, 2015. www.forbes.com.
2. Quoted in Jason Belzer, "Sports Industry 101: Breaking into the Business of Sports," *Forbes*, February 5, 2014. www.forbes.com.

Athletic Trainer

3. Casey Riley, "What Does It Take to Be an Athletic Trainer?," *Advocate-Messenger*, March 31, 2017. www.amnews.com.
4. Riley, "What Does It Take to Be an Athletic Trainer?"
5. Katie Lemmon, "Keeping Dancers Dancing," NATA News, April 2014. www.nata.org.

Coach

6. Quoted in Brian McCallum, "Q&A: New Satellite High Football Coach Ted Kimmey," *Florida Today*, April 17, 2017. www.floridatoday.com.
7. Alan Goldberg, "What Makes a Good Coach?," Competitive Advantage, 2017. www.competitivedge.com.
8. Goldberg, "What Makes a Good Coach?"
9. Quoted in Brett McKay and Kate McKay, "So You Want My Job: NBA Strength and Conditioning Coach," Art of Manliness, August 4, 2011. www.artofmanliness.com.
10. Quoted in "Coaching Q&A: Women's National Team Head Coach Jill Ellis," US Soccer, July 7, 2014. www.ussoccer.com.

Sports Physical Therapist

11. Jon Herting, "How to Become a Sports Physical Therapist," Sports Rehab and Performance Group, April 30, 2014. http://sportsrehabandperformancegroup.org.
12. Mike Reinold, "5 Tips for Landing a Sports Medicine Job in Professional Sports," Mike Reinold.com, 2017. https://mikereinold.com/landing-job-in-professional-sports.
13. Mike Reinold, "5 Tips for Landing a Sports Medicine Job in Professional Sports."

Sports Statistician

14. Quoted in Jim Albert, "Preparing for a Career as a Sports Statistician: Two Interviews with People in the Field," Stattrak, August 1, 2012. http://stattrak.amstat.org.
15. Brad Johnson, "How Bookmakers Make Money," Gambling Sites, 2017. www.gamblingsites.org.
16. Quoted in Albert, "Preparing for a Career as a Sports Statistician."
17. Rebecca Nichols, "Internship Opportunities Listing Form for Organizations," American Statistical Association, 2017. www.amstat.org.
18. Quoted in Dennis Viloria, "Sports Statistical Analyst," Bureau of Labor Statistics, September 2015. www.bls.gov.
19. Quoted in Viloria, "Sports Statistical Analyst."
20. Quoted in Albert, "Preparing for a Career as a Sports Statistician."

Sports Nutritionist

21. Steve Weatherford, "What an Average NFL Player Eats During Training Camp, According to the League's Fittest Punter," *USA Today*, August 27, 2015. http://ftw.usatoday.com.
22. Quoted in Cal Powell, "Fueling the Dawgs: A Q&A with a UGA Sports Nutritionist," University of Georgia, September 18, 2015. www.fcs.uga.edu.
23. Quoted in Sarah Klein, "NFL Nutritionist on Why Healthy Eating Makes Champions," *Huffpost*, February 1, 2014. www.huffingtonpost.com.
24. Quoted in Rebecca Rehm, "Q&A with Sports Dietician Kate Moran," *Naples Illustrated*, March 2, 2017. www.naplesillustrated.com.
25. Quoted in Powell, "Fueling the Dawgs."
26. Quoted in Powell, "Fueling the Dawgs."

Sporting Event Planner

27. Quoted in Libby Hoppe, "Q&A: Mike Duhon, National Cheerleaders Association," Connect Sports, June 18, 2013. www.connectsports.com.
28. Quoted in Hoppe, "Q&A: Mike Duhon, National Cheerleaders Association."
29. Quoted in Timothy Magaw, "Q&A: Anne Siegel, Manager of Fundraising Events, Rock and Roll Hall of Fame," *Crain's Cleveland Business*, March 18, 2017. www.crainscleveland.com.
30. Nicola Briggs, "The Life of a Corporate Event Planner," *Main Event Corporate* (blog), March, 22, 2016. www.maineventcorporate.com.au.
31. Quoted in Magaw, "Q&A: Anne Siegel, Manager of Fundraising Events, Rock and Roll Hall of Fame."
32. Quoted in Magaw, "Q&A: Anne Siegel, Manager of Fundraising Events, Rock and Roll Hall of Fame."
33. Alison Kasko, "What They Didn't Tell You About Becoming an Event Planner," *Pointers for Planners* (blog), November 1, 2016. https://blog.qceventplanning.com.

Umpire/Referee

34. Quoted in Jared Bell, "Q&A: MLB Umpire Adam Hamari," *News Tribune* (La Salle, IL), August 7, 2013. www.newstrib.com.
35. Quoted in John Clayton, "Refereeing Can Often Be Full-Time Job," ESPN, September 5, 2016. http://static.espn.go.com.
36. Quoted in Grant Hughes, "The Secret Life of NBA Referees," *Bleacher Report*, August 20, 2013. http://bleacherreport.com.
37. Quoted in Champayne Bodie, "Rising Demand for College Officials," *Bulletin* (Emporia State University), April 28, 2017. www.esubulletin.com.

Sports Speech Therapist

38. Quoted in Stuttering Foundation, "Sproles Joins Stuttering Foundation," 2016. www.stutteringhelp.org.
39. Jim D. Moss, "The Role of Speech Therapists in Treating Concussions," *Intermountain Healthcare* (blog), October 2, 2014. https://intermountainhealthcare.org.
40. Amika Osumi, "Ithaca College Athletic Trainer Teams with Speech Therapist to Help Athletes Breathe Better," NCC News, August 6, 2015. https://nccnews.expressions.syr.edu.
41. Quoted in Shelly D. Hutchins, "Head Games," AHSA Leader, October 2016. http://leader.pubs.asha.org.
42. Quoted in Juliet Farmer, "20 Questions: Kimberly O. Scanlon, SLP," Student Doctor Network, February 12, 2012. www.studentdoctor.net.

INTERVIEW WITH A SPORTS NUTRITIONIST

Tovah Segelman is a certified group fitness instructor and sports nutritionist. Her work focuses on integrating fitness, food, and health. She answered these questions by e-mail.

Q: How long have you been a sports nutritionist?

A: I have been working in the field of fitness for over 6 years and added in the nutrition piece of my profession about 2 years ago. I find the combination of being a fitness professional and nutrition consultant is the best way to help people to reach their personal health goals.

Q: Why did you become a sports nutritionist?

A: I was working as a group fitness instructor and found that many people who were taking my classes were looking for guidance with their nutrition. They wanted to know what foods to eat and not eat, what size portions, what protein powders to use, what supplements to take.

Q: How is working with athletes different from working with nonathletic clients?

A: Athletes and non-athletes have very different concerns and different goals. Athletes need to perform, they need to prevent injury, and they need to make sure that they are fueling their bodies for optimal performance. Professional athletes and Olympic athletes need to be careful about what supplements they take because of the stringent blood tests from the International Olympic Committee (IOC) so it's important to understand the purity of vitamins and protein powders you recommend to them. For non-athletic clients their diets need to be balanced differently because they are not as active and require less carbohydrates.

Q: What types of sports do your athletic clients participate in?

A: Right now I have a mix of clients—some are runners, some are triathletes, and the majority are more daily exercisers who take my fitness classes such as bootcamp, weightlifting, and yoga classes.

Q: Can you describe your typical workday?

A: That's the best part of being your own boss! In a typical day I get up and go teach a fitness class and then spend some time . . . with my team to brainstorm about upcoming events, workshops, or webinars we could offer. Most of the nutrition counseling I can do from my home, in a coffee shop, or even on vacation! It goes with me wherever I go!

Q: What are the most rewarding aspects of your job?

A: Receiving texts and messages from my clients about how much better they feel and seeing their health improvements, which include improved bone density, reduced blood sugar levels, weight loss, improved muscle strength, improved athletic performance, improved energy levels, improved digestion, reduced inflammation, reduced allergy symptoms, improved hair, skin, and nails, and the list goes on!!

Q: What are the biggest challenges you face in your job?

A: As much as I love the freedom and flexibility of my schedule, at the same time it can be hard to be "on call" all the time. I can receive a message at any time of day from a client asking a question, asking to place an order, etc. This isn't a 9-5 desk job; you have to be there to support your clients when they need you, nights, weekends, anytime. There is always someone to check on, someone new to reach out to and offer to help, another social media post I could do, another article I could share. So you need to sometimes define your "work time" so you can also balance it with some relaxation and down time.

Q: What personal qualities do you find most valuable for this type of work?

A: Definitely being outgoing and friendly is a huge asset. You have to have strong communication skills, be comfortable speaking in front of groups, be confident in what you are sharing or educating about. You can't let fear hold you back. You have to be a go-getter and get out there and market yourself and your business. Most importantly, you have to be willing to be vulnerable and share your own personal successes and struggles. People like when I share my struggles with food and that I'm human just like them.

Q: What advice do you have for students who might be interested in becoming a sports nutritionist?

A: Focus on your WHY. Your deep down WHY. Not "I want to make money" or "I want to help others." What really drives you? If you can connect with your WHY, you will be successful in whatever professional area you choose. What is going to get you out of bed and excited to go to "work" every day? What are you passionate about? Follow your passion and your WHY and you'll never "work" a day in your life.

Q: What is something about your job that you think would surprise most people?

A: It's a lot more work than people think! People are surprised when I tell them I'm looking up workouts online and coming up with class sequences or that I'm on at least 1 webinar/week, usually more, to learn about how I can best help others and how to grow my business, or that I'm having team meetings and team phone calls.

Q: What were your favorite subjects in school?

A: In high school I was a math and science person. I loved math, and especially loved biology and anatomy. Now I'm also a language person, I recognize how important communication is, I love motivational quotes, and recognize how important listening is in helping others.

OTHER CAREERS IF YOU LIKE SPORTS

Caddy
Camp director
Director of Minor League
   Operations
Equipment manager
Exercise physiologist
Fitness program coordinator
Kinesiotherapist
Marketing and promotions
   coordinator
Medical assistant
Physical education instructor
Recreation worker
Scoreboard operator
Scout
Sports agent
Sports engineer
Sports journalist

Sports lawyer
Sports massage therapist
Sports physician
Sports psychologist
Sports public relations
   assistant
Sports sales representative
Sports scientist
Sporting goods store manager
Sporting goods salesperson
Sportscaster
Stadium manager
Television sports producer
Therapeutic recreation director
Ticket operations manager
Wellness manager
Youth sports administrator

Editor's note: The online *Occupational Outlook Handbook* of the US Department of Labor's Bureau of Labor Statistics is an excellent source of information on jobs in hundreds of career fields, including many of those listed here. The *Occupational Outlook Handbook* may be accessed online at www.bls.gov/ooh.

INDEX